# What Do You Mean
# I Can't Write?

## A practical guide to business writing
## for agency account managers

### By Norm MacMaster

ISBN-10: 1-887229-29-9
ISBN-13: 978-1-887229-29-6

**The Copy Workshop**
a division of Bruce Bendinger Creative Communications, Inc.
2144 N Hudson
Chicago, IL 60614
773.871.1179
thecopyworkshop@aol.com

*To Maureen, Scott and Christine —*
*my principal teachers over the years.*

# Table of contents         Page

# I  Introduction

*"What do you mean I can't write..."*

That was my reaction the first time someone criticized my writing. It might be your reaction too. But if you're like most people in business, the truth is you don't write as well as you should.

Good writing skills have been drilled out of you by a thousand bad habits and influences—e-mail and text messaging to name just two.

In many ways, your writing was best when you were a child.

The writing of grade school children is invariably direct and understandable. That's because their perceptions are clear, their concepts simple, and their self-expression uninhibited.

The purpose of this book, then, is to help you regain your lost youth—at least in terms of your writing style.

We'll do this by giving you a series of practical suggestions you can apply to any writing task to make your communication more explicit and concise. You'll find these tips in the next chapter.

Then, subsequent chapters will give you specific directions on how to write the different types of letters, memos, and recommendations that are expected of you as an advertising professional.

The last chapter of this guide is unwritten.

It will be written by you as you practice, practice, and practice to break the bad writing habits picked up during your lifetime.

While this guide will improve your ability to write, it will not improve your grammar. There are many excellent books designed to do that.

One of the best is *The Elements of Style* by William J. Strunk and E.B. White. You should have a copy within reach at all times.

This guide will not make you a creative writer. That's a talent that can be perfected but not acquired, although there are many similarities between effective copywriting and effective business writing.

Good writing skills are a prerequisite for success in advertising. This guide will help you succeed.

Peggy Noonan, President Reagan's superb speech writer, once remarked on how sensitive Reagan was when editing her work because he knew that "...I was new and trying."

I've also benefited from dozens of people who took the time to review, critique and improve my writing during the course of my career.

To each of these unidentified mentors I send my deepest thanks. You know who you are.

# II  Sixteen tips to improve your writing, now!

Writing is not an excuse to flaunt your vocabulary or exercise your ability for infinite speculation on a finite subject. In most instances, business writing is about persuading.

In this sense, business writing is a first cousin to copywriting. And the rules for effective advertising apply with full force.

At the turn of the century (not the last one, the one before that) the most successful copywriter in America was a man by the name of Claude Hopkins. (He wrote a book entitled *Scientific Advertising*; you should read it.)

Here's what Hopkins had to say about the style of a good copywriter:

> *"One must be able to express himself briefly, clearly and convincingly, just as a salesman must. But fine writing is a distinct disadvantage. So is unique literary style. They take attention from the subject."*

These words also describe the style of an effective business writer and explain why it is wrong to use seldom-understood words or to write in a pretentious manner.

Another great ad man from the past was Fairfax Cone (he was one of the founders of Foote, Cone and Belding). See how Cone's five essential ingredients of good advertising apply to business writing:

> *"It is the primary requirement of advertising to be clear, clear as to exactly what the proposition is."*

So it is with business writing!

*"The second essential of advertising is that what must be clear must also be important. The proposition must have hard value."*

How many memos have you seen that violate this principle. Memos written for the self-satisfaction of the writer, at the reader's expense.

*"Third, the proposition that is both clear and important must also have a personal appeal. It should be beamed at its logical prospects; no one else matters."*

If more people followed this rule, the number of memos and e-mails you receive each day would be cut at least in half. So often we're copied on subjects that hold no interest for us. Use the "Reply All" button on your computer sparingly.

*"Fourth, good advertising expresses the personality of the advertiser."*

Business writing, like copywriting, is a substitute for talking to someone person to person.

Let your personality show through. Write as you speak.

*"Finally, a good advertisement demands action.*
*"It asks for an order or it exacts a mental pledge."*

The majority of all memos and e-mails fail on this point, either because of laziness or timidity. If more memos asked for the order, more would be accomplished in less time. And that would be progress.

To sum up, writing is persuading—this is true whether it's copywriting or business writing.

Now here are sixteen tips to help you write more persuasively.

# 1. Start with an outline

Just as successful advertising starts with a strategy, successful business writing starts with an outline.

- What is it you wish to say to your readers?
- What points must you make?
- What do you want your readers to do?
- What information must they have before they'll do what you want them to do?

The answers to these and similar questions make up your outline. Put them in some logical order and you have a map to follow as you write. Without a map, you'll get lost. And if you get lost, just think where your readers will be! As Yogi Berra once said "If you don't know where you're going, you could end up some place else."

**Example:**

This is an outline for a letter to a client confirming the details of a new product assignment.

- Opening paragraph—express thanks for the assignment and for the confidence the client has shown in your agency.
- Next, define the assignment.
- Then, identify the major issues and priorities
- Set a broad timetable for dealing with these issues.
- Identify the agency personnel assigned to the project.
- Outline the remuneration agreement.
- Outline the next steps and timing.
- Close by again expressing your gratitude.

## 2. Be clear

Your meaning must be clear on first reading.

Your audience has neither the time nor patience to speculate on what you meant to say.

If your meaning isn't clear, you will be misunderstood and you will fail to persuade. E.B.White says;

> *"When you have said something, make sure you have said it. The chances of your having said it are only fair."*

**Example:**

| Wrong | Right |
|---|---|
| Developments that appear to be in the distant future, will, in eighteen months, be a mere two years off | Developments that seem a long way off will occur faster than we think. |

Speaking about political campaigns, a famous New York City politician observed, "If you must explain what you are trying to say, you've got a problem."

## 3. Be simple

The best way to write clearly is to write simply.

Simple ideas are the most powerful; simple thoughts the most profound.

Some people think, mistakenly, that they demonstrate their intelligence when they write in a complex, often obtuse manner or with a style so florid it borders on Old English.

This is not a sign of intelligence.

It's a sign of egotism, of disdain for your audience.

It is not persuasive writing.

**Example:**

| Wrong | Right |
|---|---|
| Coincident with the occurrence of the vernal equinox, the imagination of the males of the species tend to be dominated by amorous considerations. | In Spring, a young man's fancy turns to thoughts of love. |

# 4. Be short

The best way to write simply is to use short words. The most powerful words are short words. Love. Hate. Birth. Death. Use short sentences and short paragraphs.

Churchill said:

*"The best words are small words.*
*And old, small words are the best of all."*

**Example:**

| Use | Instead of |
|---|---|
| See | Envision |
| Urge | Encourage |
| Help | Facilitate |
| Fire | Terminate |
| Fat | Overweight |

Short sentences are better than long sentences.

Remember this basic rule: one sentence, one thought.

Break up ninety percent of all compound sentences into simple sentences using the subject/predicate/object sentence structure. Your writing style will improve immediately.

**Example:**

| Wrong | Right |
|---|---|
| While the brand's media budget has been increased each year for the past five years, the brand has not enjoyed the benefits of these increases in the form of increased advertising support as they have been more than offset by inflation. | The brand's media budget has increased annually for the past five years. However, this has not resulted in more advertising support. These increases have been wiped out by media inflation |

Short sentences make short paragraphs.

Short paragraphs make short memos.

Short memos get read!

Here's a thought from Ernest Hemingway on keeping it short:

*"My temptation is always to write too much. I keep it under control so as not to have to cut out crap and re-write. Guys who think they are geniuses because they have never learned how to say no to a typewriter are a common phenomenon. All you have to do is get a phony style and you can write any amount of words."*

## 5. Be specific

Use concrete nouns that are packed with meaning.

Ambiguous words permit, even invite, misinterpretation.

You won't persuade if you're misinterpreted.

For example, rather than saying "The brand's second quarter promotion was judged to be a success...," define what you mean by "a success." Did the promotion exceed its goals? By how much? What trial levels did it generate? What redemption rates were achieved? How many units were sold?

Similarly, don't simply say, "High television production costs are seen as a problem for the brand..." Define the problem. Will you need to develop a new, less expensive creative approach? Will you need to consider other media? Will you need to transfer money from elsewhere in the budget to fund the television production?

Limit your use of adjectives. Strong nouns seldom need the help of adjectives; weak nouns always do.

Voltaire said, "The adjective is the enemy of the noun." An excessive use of adjectives signifies either an ornate writing style or laziness. . It is laziness when you opt for a weak noun that needs propping up by an adjective rather than searching for a strong noun that can stand on its own.

## 6. Avoid clichés, legalese and businessese

Write English. Clichés have no punch.

Legalese is incomprehensible except to others of the same bent.

And businessese is purposely obtuse.

Here are a few words and phrases to avoid:

> Input
> Interface
> Time frame
> The big picture
> The bottom line
> For all intents and purposes
> Give me your perspective
> Enlighten me on this

# 7. Stamp out motherhood

Motherhood statements are like little white lies.

They are designed to take the edge off the truth—either because the write wishes to please everyone by avoiding contentious issues or because the writer is too lazy to develop strong arguments to bolster contentious positions. Motherhood statements smother ideas.

## 8. Write actively

Use active rather than passive verbs.

Active verbs add vigor and pace to your writing.

Passive verbs put people to sleep.

**Example:**

| Say | Rather Than |
|---|---|
| Everyone knows… | It's a well-known fact… |
| The research group believes… | The research group is of the opinion… |
| This commercial broke all test records. | This is the highest scoring commercial we've ever tested. |
| Competitive brands dominate our fourth place brand. | Our brand is fourth in the market and trails all competitive brands by a good margin. |
| The enemies of free speech attack advertising. | Advertising is being attacked by the enemies of free speech. |

Write with confidence.

Replace the cowardly phrase, *"The research suggests that we should…"* with an assertive statement, *"Based on the research, we should…."*

## 9. Be concise

Don't write rambling sentences with ideas that roam from paragraph to paragraph. Compress your thoughts into as few words as possible.

If two letters arrive on your desk simultaneously, one of four or five paragraphs, the other four pages long, which one will you read first?

Remember this when you write your next letter.

## 10. Be easy to follow

Give your readers a break. Give them directions.

Long memos and letters should start with a summary of the thoughts that follow.

Then, use headings and sub heads freely to act as signposts, guiding your reader through your logic.

Long sections should be broken up by numbering important paragraphs.

Supplemental points, explaining or supporting a main point, should also be numbered.

Start each paragraph with a topic sentence, then elaborate on this thought for the rest of the paragraph.

Where possible, end each paragraph with a bridging sentence to guide the reader to the next paragraph.

## 11. Art direct your writing

This will make your writing more readable.

Indent sentences or whole paragraphs for emphasis.

Underline <u>key words</u> to drive home your point.
- Use bullets for secondary or supporting points.

Avoid capitalization. Lower case is more readable.

Letters, like advertisements, benefit from white space.

Use wide margins and double space between paragraphs.

## 12. Spell correctly

Nothing is more distracting than a misspelled word.

Frequent spelling mistakes reflect sloppy writing.

Sloppy writing is a sign of sloppy thinking.

Sloppy thinking is not persuasive.

## 13. Use proper grammar

All that was said for errors in spelling applies equally to errors in grammar.

## 14. Use symbols, abbreviations and acronyms sparingly

Not all symbols are universally known.

Many, such as the percent sign (%), are unsightly when surrounded by words.

The best policy is to use words, not symbols.

The same is true of abbreviations.

If you must use acronyms, at least explain their meaning the first time you use them.

As for numbers, write them out from zero to ten.

Use digits for 11 and above.

Cryptic codes and abbreviations are fine for text messaging, but they have no place in more formal communications, even e-mail.

## 15. Edit ruthlessly

The pace of your writing will improve immediately.

Rearrange sentences so that the point you wish to emphasize is at the end of the sentence. Cut all needless words.

The first to go should be such useless adverbs as "really," "seriously," "very," "timely," "lovely," "nice." An excessive use of adverbs, like an excessive use of adjectives, shows you are either lazy or pretentious.

Next, cut all stilted phrases.

**Example:**

| Use | Instead of |
| --- | --- |
| about | with regard to |
| like | along the lines of |
| if | in the event that |
| to | in order to; with a view to |
| for | for the purpose of |
| about | in the neighborhood of |

# 16. Draft and re-draft

Every piece of writing will improve with a second and third draft.

Let some time elapse between your re-writes. Then you'll be able to approach the task with fresh thinking.

Let other people review your drafts. They'll be more objective in their criticism.

Remember the advice of Samuel Johnson:

> *"Read your compositions and when you meet a passage which you think is particularly fine, strike it out."*

Follow these 16 suggestions and you will communicate more clearly, write more persuasively, and achieve more success.

Ignore them and you will limit your effectiveness with your client and within your agency.

---

**Three Ways To Make Sure No One Reads What You Write**

- Use long, complicated sentences that go on...and...on...and...on...and...on...endlessly. Your readers will become confused and disoriented. They will quickly forget the point you were trying to make when the sentence began. Eventually, they will give up and do something else.
- Include as many clichés as possible. This tells your readers you have nothing new to say and have put no thought whatever into your writing. They will conclude there is no need to read further.
- Include all possible details no matter how trivial or marginally relevant. This will sap your readers' interest and attention, tiring them out. They will soon seek relief by reading something more interesting.

# III How to write analyses

If there's one ability that is fundamental to successful business writing it's the ability to write a perceptive analysis. Recommendations stand or fall on the basis of their supporting analysis.

Strategies can be insightful or mundane depending on the analysis upon which they're built. Even store check reports or competitive copy assessments require thorough analysis for excellence.

An analysis should contain three distinct sections:

- The *background* section where you *report* the facts that are available.
- The *conclusions* section where you *interpret* the facts for your reader.
- The *recommendations* section where you specify the *action to be taken* based on your interpretation of the facts.

Poor analysis writing results from either omitting one of these sections or from mixing them together to the bewilderment of your reader.

In this section, we will give you some tips on how to write analyses that are complete, insightful, and action-oriented.

## Background

This is the first section of your analysis. Here, you report on all the facts available—objectively and dispassionately.

The most common mistake made in this section is to interject opinion and interpretation. Save this for later. For now, just give us the facts.

Here are nine tips to help you do this.

## 1. Gather all the facts

Start by listing all the possible factors that should be included in your analysis. Then, surround yourself with the resources that will provide the facts for each item.

Don't start writing until you have every resource no more than an arm's length away. Otherwise, you'll interrupt your writing by searching for information and this will slow your progress.

## 2. Check with others

Once you've listed all the factors you plan to analyze, ask your colleagues if they have any additions to suggest. This is particularly crucial if your analysis must be approved by someone else. Nothing is more frustrating for you, and for the approver, than to re-write an analysis because three or four factors were omitted. Avoid this by having the approver review your outline of factors before you begin to write.

## 3. Arrange your facts in logical order

Some find it difficult to construct a logical order for their analysis. It shouldn't be. The rule is very simple: Proceed from the most general or common to the most specific or unique.

For example, when writing a market analysis, start by describing the performance of the market as a whole, then move to the performance of the category and then your brand and its competition. Begin with the largest geographic unit and proceed to the smallest. When writing a research analysis, start by describing broad performance measures and end by discussing the performance of your brand on specific attribute ratings.

## 4. Label your assumptions

Because of a lack of facts, you may need to include assumptions or theories in your background section. This is permissible provided they are labeled as such. Don't try to hide them under euphemisms such as *"experience suggests…"* or, *"conventional wisdom has it…."* Come right out and say, *"We believe that…"* or *"On judgment…."* Be confident.

### 5.  Keep it simple

The first sentence of each section should state the basic observation being made in that section. Subsequent sentences merely elaborate on this fact.

Know what to omit. Not every fact merits comment.

If a fact has only marginal impact on your conclusions or recommended action, leave it out.

### 6.  Keep it objective

No embellishments please. The background section should contain only your dispassionate observations. Few adjectives or adverbs should appear in this section. Save your veiled, self-congratulatory remarks ("The brand surged ahead by half a share point after the advertising broke…") for the cover letter.

### 7.  Keep to the facts

No conclusions in this section. Mixing facts with conclusions is one of the most common mistakes in writing analyses.

### 8.  Store numbers in exhibits

Use statistical tables sparingly in your report. Put them in an exhibit section and simply refer to them in your text. If you must include tables within the text, don't verbalize what is clearly communicated by the numbers. This defeats the purpose. Let the numbers speak for themselves and use the text to make a broader, perhaps more unifying observation about what is shown.

## 9. Construct simple exhibits

Statistical exhibits should be constructed with the same care used to construct a sentence. Limit the number of variables you deal with to four at most. For example, when showing the volume trends for a group of brands include only the absolute volume and annual percentage change for each brand for each year as shown below.

### Annual Volume Trends
### 2003-2005
### (MM Widgets)

| | 2003 | | 2004 | | 2005 | |
|---|---|---|---|---|---|---|
| | Units | % Chge. | Units | % Chge. | Units | % Chge. |
| Brand A | 100.0 | 10 | 120.0 | 20 | 126.0 | 5 |
| Brand B | 90.0 | 5 | 99.0 | 10 | 103.9 | 5 |
| Brand C | 50.0 | 20 | 75.0 | 50 | 90.0 | 20 |

Sources: XYZ Industry Statistics

Do not try to include the brands' shares as well, as these constitute a fifth point that will only make your exhibit confusing.

# Conclusions

In this second section, you take the facts previously reported as discrete bits of information and use your knowledge, experience and intuition to combine and interpret them for your reader.

For example, if you were analyzing the operation of a clock, you would have described the individual parts of the clock in the first section. In the conclusions section, you would tell your reader how the individual pieces work together to make the clock function.

Here are four tips to help you do this.

### 1. Follow your plan

Use the same logical sequence used in the background section. Start from the broadest conclusion and proceed to the most specific.

### 2. Combine facts

In the background section, you limited your focus to each fact independently. Your observation was linear. Now you should adopt a helicopter perspective and try to see the whole picture. You're looking for complementary facts, emerging patterns, cause and effect relationships, synergy. Some facts will be combined to reach broad conclusions. Others will be used to explain the occurrence or absence of phenomena.

### 3. Use your experience

This is the creative part of your analysis. Use your knowledge and experience to interpret the facts. Do they form a pattern that parallels sound advertising or marketing principles? Do they contradict such principles? Is there a cause and effect relationship that supports basic advertising guidelines? Or contradicts such guidelines? Does the pattern of facts resemble others you've observed or learned about in different markets? If so, based on what happened in those other markets what do you think will happen here?

### 4. Be authoritative

State your conclusions with confidence. Don't vacillate or equivocate. There's no need to be timid if you've studied the facts thoroughly, reported them objectively, and used your experience to help identify underlying patterns. Don't waffle. And don't be afraid to be wrong.

---

**Three Ways To Have Your Analyses Rejected**

- Purposely or inadvertently omit two or three important facts from your analysis. By not identifying all the key facts to be covered before you begin to write, you can be sure to overlook some and give your readers an excuse to toss out your analysis as incomplete.
- Show your bias early and often. Make sure your readers know which side of the issue you're on so they can skip your analysis in favor of a more objective approach if they are pressed for time.
- Avoid drawing any conclusions. This will save you considerable time and effort. After all, can't your readers connect the dots?

---

# Recommendations

This is the final section of your analysis, where you draw the preceding sections together by specifying what action should be taken.

Here's where many otherwise well-written analyses falter.

The writer yields the initiative by not specifying what needs to be done. He lazily leaves it to the reader to deduce this for himself.

Unfortunately, the writer doesn't realize his efforts to report and interpret the facts are wasted if no action is taken.

Every analysis should include recommendations for further action.

It's true that often the analysis will form the basis for a broader, more formal recommendation that may be prepared by another person or work unit.

Nevertheless, always make sure that readers of your analyses know what you think should be done next.

The secrets to writing cogent recommendation sections are simple:

- **First**, make your recommendations fit your conclusions. (They should flow directly from your conclusions and follow the same logical pattern established in the preceding sections.)

- **Second**, state precisely what action you are recommending.

- **Third**, as in all matters, specify who should carry out each recommendation and when this should be done. Leave nothing to chance!

# IV   How to write formal recommendations

Recommendations are the way you move your client's business ahead and ensure the growth of your agency.

If you are unable to write persuasive recommendations, you will not bring success to your client, your agency or yourself. As you can see from the previous paragraphs, a recommendation is simply the logical extension of an analysis.

If you become a skilled analyst, writing formal recommendations will be effortless.

A recommendation consists of four parts:

- The **background** section.
- The **recommendation** itself.
- The **discussion** of the recommendation.
- The **next steps** required.

### The importance of the topical sentence

Please note that while the detailed explanation of your recommendation comes in the second section, you must succinctly tell the reader the purpose of your letter or memo in the opening paragraph.

*"This letter recommends that we conduct an online advertising test with Google and Yahoo during the second quarter of this year."*

## Background

You walk a tightrope when writing the background section of your recommendation. On one hand, you realize your reader lacks your knowledge of the subject and that you must use this section to educate him or her. On the other hand, don't overload your reader with inconsequential facts. This will only make your recommendation longer than necessary and confuse, even annoy, your audience.

As you write the background section, continually apply the test of relevance to each fact that you include.

The background section is a distillation of the first two sections of an analysis. You summarize all pertinent facts and give your interpretation of these as well. All the guidelines given for writing analyses apply here. However, three points should be emphasized:

### 1.  Be objective
Any hint of bias will cause your reader to be skeptical. Skeptical audiences are hard to persuade.

### 2.  Have a logical order
Lead your reader through your thinking in a step-by-step manner.

### 3.  Use headings and numbers freely
Erect all manner of signposts to make life easier for your reader.

## Recommendation

Here, you outline the essential details of your recommendation. Include details such as:

- The purpose of the recommendation.
- What costs are involved.
- When the recommendation is to be executed.
- Where...
- How...
- And by whom.

In short, you give your reader a précis of the recommendation, which provides the details needed to comprehend the discussion of the recommendation that follows.

# Discussion

This section will generally have two sub-sections:

- The basis for the recommendation.
- The details of the recommendation.

The purpose of the first section is to persuade your audience to accept your recommendation. You must argue for its acceptance by:

- *Explaining* how it is an appropriate solution to the problems or opportunities identified in the background section.

- *Objectively assessing* the recommendation's strengths and weaknesses plus the trade-offs it entails. (All decisions or recommendations require trade-offs. Where these are significant, you can increase the credibility of your case by identifying and assessing them for your reader.)

- *Describing and evaluating* alternative approaches which you considered and rejected. (Your assessment of these should help show the correctness of your recommended approach.)

- *Demonstrating* how what you are recommending is in keeping with established business principles, commonly accepted best practices, agreed to lessons learned or how it is analogous to the successful practices of other brands in other categories.

- *Anticipating* questions or barriers to acceptance and addressing these in advance.

*Objectivity* is key to this section. View your recommendation and alternatives from all perspectives, then give your reader your considered and unbiased assessment to help him reach a decision. Objectivity will increase your credibility and credibility is a prerequisite for persuasion.

The purpose of the second part of your discussion section is to elaborate on the details of your recommendation. You gain the confidence of your reader by showing that you have considered all aspects of the recommendation and how it will be executed.

Be complete. Many sound recommendations have died because the writer failed to describe fully their implementation. The reader either couldn't or wouldn't imagine how the abstract recommendation could be transformed into concrete action.

## Next steps

The purpose of this final section is to breathe life into your recommendation by spelling out exactly what needs to be done next, by whom and with whose permission. By doing this, you create momentum for your recommendation. It's easier to say no to a project that hasn't begun than it is to reject a project that seems to have a life of its own.

---

**Three Ways To Have Your Recommendations Ignored**

- Skip the background section. After all, if your readers aren't up to speed on the issues it's not your fault.
- Be assiduously evenhanded. Use a lot of "On the one hand....but on the other hand..." sentences. What ever you do, don't give the appearance of taking a position. Ambiguity is a virtue.
- Stop short of suggesting any action. Why go out on the limb any more than you have already? Besides, others might have a better idea than you on what should be done next.

---

# V    How to write strategies

Strategies are possibly the documents advertising people write most poorly. This is unfortunate as they are also the most crucial documents they write.

Strategies guide our efforts at each stage of the marketing process.

Here's what Jay Chiat had to say about advertising strategies:

> *"Our best work has always begun with a marketing solution, not a creative solution. The ads flowed from the Strategy, not the Strategy from the ads."*

To be effective, strategies must be clear, precise, and based on fact plus sound judgments.

Many people confuse strategies with objectives or even with tactics. The following definitions should clear things up.

- Objectives state what you wish to accomplish in measurable terms.

- Strategies describe how you will accomplish your objectives, most often in abstract terms.

- Tactics define the specific execution of your strategies in concrete terms. The whens, wheres, whys and what fors. A media plan is a tactical document. So is a storyboard or a research proposal.

Winston Churchill gave us a succinct definition of objectives and strategies when he said:

> *"My objective is victory. My strategy is to wage war."*

Advertising people must be able to write three types of strategies:

- Marketing strategies
- Media strategies
- Creative strategies

We will give you tips on writing each of these.

## A. Marketing strategies

The marketing strategy is the brand's operational blueprint.

It defines what the brand is to achieve and how each marketing weapon will be used to achieve this.

Here are nine ways to write better marketing strategies.

### 1. Use a logical format

Here's a marketing strategy format that works. When a client doesn't have a format of his own, use this one.

- Marketing objectives and goals
- Source of volume
- Target group (demographic and psychographic descriptions)
- Product strategy
- Pricing strategy
- Media strategy
- Internet strategy
- Copy strategy
- Packaging strategy
- Promotion strategy
- Research strategy
- Channel strategy

## 2. Define your objectives properly

Marketing objectives tell what the brand is expected to achieve in the coming year in terms of the growth, stability, or decline of its absolute dollar volume or share.

There are only nine marketing objective options available to a brand at any time. They can be easily described in the following matrix:

| Marketing Objective Options | Absolute Volume | Financial Volume | Share |
|---|---|---|---|
| Increase | | | |
| Hold Stable | | | |
| Minimize Decline | | | |

A brand cannot have, as a marketing objective, any of the following:

- To introduce a line extension.
  This is a tactical execution of the brand's product strategy.
- To increase awareness.
  This may be the goal of the media and copy strategies.
- To increase trial.
  This may be the goal of the promotion strategy.

## 3. Identify your source of volume

If your marketing objective is to maintain volume or minimize declines, your source of volume (except in rare instances) will be your current users. If your objective is to increase volume, your source of incremental volume can be only one or a combination of:

- Increased consumption from current users.
- Conversion of competitive brand users to your brand.
- Conversion of non-users to the category and your brand.

When defining the user group, be specific.

What type of current users will increase consumption—light, medium or heavy users? Which competitive brand's users will you convert? And are they light, medium or heavy users?

If you plan to bring non-users into the category, what do these consumers currently use in place of your product?

### 4. Tell how your incremental volume will be obtained

This is the second part of your source of volume statement.

Here's a checklist to help you make this determination.

- Will you cause current users to increase consumption of your product by using more of it at each occasion? Or will they use your product more frequently?
- If you want them to use it more frequently, will they use it in much the same way they do now or will they use it in new ways or at new occasions? On what basis will they be persuaded to do this?
- Will they use your product in place of another? If so, what product will be replaced and why?
- Will competitive brand users switch to your brand exclusively? If so, why?
- Will they continue with their current brand primarily and use your brand as an alternative? When? Why?
- On what basis will you persuade non-users to enter the category?
- What products will they use less of in order to consume your product?
- On what basis will they make this substitution?

### 5. Define your target group precisely

Most target group descriptions are motherhood statements. They don't define a target; they define a group.

A target is a point of focus.

A target group is the single largest, most homogeneous group of consumers you wish to reach with your advertising to cause the most significant degree of change.

"Women 18 to 49" is not a target group. There is no homogeneity. The 18 to 25 year olds have little in common with the 45 to 49 year olds.

Some argue that a broad target group definition is required to identify those consumers who account for the majority of the brand's volume. This is specious reasoning. The target group defines only the group you will key on. It does not suggest you will ignore all other groups.

Properly defining a target group requires trade-offs.

But clarity of thought always requires sacrifices; the general for the specific; the abstract for the concrete; the ambiguous for the precise.

## 6. Define your target group fully

The demographic terms used should conform to the common groupings used in marketing and media research. If these are too general for your product (for example, a luxury product purchased primarily by women with household incomes of $300,000 plus) you must still use them for practical reasons; media planning can only be based on these general descriptions.

You can always include a supplemental definition to describe more clearly whom you really wish to reach.

Tailor the psychographic description of your target group specifically to your product. Be insightful, even intuitive in this section. This is where you must describe the attitudes and values of your target group. Their hopes, dreams, needs, wants, problems and perceptions of the world. You can't toss this off in a sentence or even two.

But don't write a book either.

### 7.  Make your strategy fit the marketing objective

This seems obvious but it's an appallingly common error.

If the objective is to increase volume by bringing non-users into the category, it's pointless to have a strategy that's directed at competitive brand users.

### 8.  Keep your strategy strategic

A strategy broadly states how a particular marketing activity will be used to achieve the brand's objective.

It does not get into the fine points of detail.

### 9.  Set goals

The achievement of most strategies can be measured.

A promotion strategy can be measured in terms of trial levels; a packaging strategy can be measured in terms of consumer preference levels; a product strategy can be measured in terms of home use test results. Set measurable goals for each strategy.

## B. Media strategies

Media strategies include more motherhood statements per line than any other document in the agency. If you follow the tips given in Chapter II you'll be able to purge such statements from your strategies.

Then follow this sequence and you will write meaningful media strategies—even in this day of new media and media proliferation.

- State your overall emphasis—reach versus frequency and the reason why you've selected this emphasis.
- Define the target group—in both demographic and psychographic terms.
- Specify the relative weight emphasis you wish by region, by city, by month, together with a rationale for this weighting.

- Specify any creative requirements.
- Specify any budget considerations.

Here are a few tips to help you further.

### 1. Avoid the best-of-both-worlds syndrome

Accurately defining your overall emphasis of reach and frequency requires trade-offs. Realize this and proceed with confidence. Make a decision! Avoid such cowardly phrases as:

*"High reach with affordable frequency."*

### 2. Fully and precisely define your target group

This is crucial.

Re-read the tips given on this subject in the previous chapter.

### 3. Involve your creative partner

Put together a media, creative and account management team to discuss what media the creative direction requires. You'll be surprised how innovative media thinking will spring from these discussions.

Often this team will generate some interesting creative thinking as well. In today's media environment, this is more important than ever.

### 4. Set goals for your media budget

The most useless phrase in any media plan goes something like this:

*"The plan must be executed within the available budget."*

Of course it must! No news here!

Your budget considerations should deal with what you want to accomplish in a competitive sense.

- A specific share of voice
- A certain share of market/share of voice ratio

• A competitive spending ratio of such and such.

These are measurable goals that will direct the planning effort more precisely.

## C. Creative strategies

Of all the memos, recommendations and strategies you'll write, creative strategies are the most important. It's the creative strategy that specifies how the agency will advertise the client's product or service. It does this by stating:

- How you want consumers to position the brand in their minds.
- What benefit you will offer consumers that will cause them to position the brand appropriately.
- What reasons you will give consumers to permit them to believe the brand delivers the benefit promised.
- What image or personality you wish to create for the brand.

If your creative strategy lacks clarity and precision ...

- The creative department will waste time producing advertising that is inappropriate.
- The client will think the agency incompetent for proposing such advertising.
- Should the client run the inappropriate advertising, his advertising budget will be wasted.
- The agency may be fired as a result.

*No other document has as much potential to enhance the agency's reputation and raise its level of productivity as does a well-written creative strategy.*

There are almost as many creative strategy formats as there are clients and agencies. It is not the purpose of this booklet to advocate one format over another. But you should be certain that the format you use allows a precise definition of the creative task.

You should also be certain that all who will use the strategy have a common understanding of the definitions inherent in that format.

Here are seven additional suggestions to help you write better strategies.

## 1. Remember your mission

The former creative leader of FCB, John O'Toole, defined advertising's mission this way:

> *"Advertising is about persons. And how a product or service fits into a person's life to make it easier, richer, better."*

Somewhere in your strategy, you should define why your prospect's life is not already easier, richer, better.

This is the problem advertising must solve.

It is *always* a consumer problem.

It is *never* a marketing problem.

Low awareness, low trial, or low brand loyalty are not the consumer problems advertising will solve.

## 2. Make trade-offs

You can't include everything in your strategy.

You must determine what is important and what isn't. This is especially true when selecting the benefit and writing the support section.

Force yourself to select only one sharply defined benefit—only one reason why your product or service will make your prospect's life easier, richer, better.

Resist the temptation to cover all the bases by including a second benefit, or by phrasing your benefit in a general way.

Be single-minded in the support section as well.

If a fact or characteristic does not have significant impact on the benefit *leave it out*.

The art of strategic thinking depends as much on knowing what to leave out as it does on knowing what to leave in.

### 3.  Be Competitive

Be sure your strategy is clear on why a consumer should select your brand over the competition.

### 4.  Keep it short and simple

If your strategy is over a page in length, it's too complex.

How can you expect your creative partners to execute in 30 seconds, something that you require two pages to describe?

### 5.  Remember your audience

The strategy is written for the benefit of your creative group - not your client. Make sure it's jargon-free and written in language everyone will understand.

### 6.  Involve the creative group

There seems to be a direct correlation between the quality of a creative strategy and the amount of involvement that creative people have had in its development.

### 7.  Inspire the creative group

The creative strategy is not a cold set of specs for some vendor—its purpose is to help some very talented people get ideas.

Find a way to inspire the creatives through your strategy. Live it up!

## 8.  Keep to one benefit

This is so important it must be repeated.

Fight to your death to have only one benefit.

It's sufficiently difficult to communicate one idea in 30 seconds, let alone two. If you *must have* two benefits (and the need for two is *always* questionable) clearly identify which is primary and which is secondary.

## 9.  No executional considerations please

These have no place in a strategy, unless they are legal requirements. In which case they should be included in the mandatories section.

You can attach a brief memo to your strategy that outlines all other items that you or your client would like considered.

But keep them out of the strategy! Their inclusion gives them an aura of legitimacy.

Great strategies, like great advertising, involve risks. The art of strategic thinking demands that you have the ability to assess risks and the courage to take them.

---

### Three Ways To Make Sure Your Creative Strategies Fail

- Insist on having more than one benefit. Media is expensive so it's cost efficient to include more than one proposition in an ad or commercial. Three might be good.
- Focus only on what your client wants to sell. Forget about consumer wants or needs. What do they know? They don't have plants to run or inventories to unload. Remember that old adage, "What's good for General Motors is good for the USA."
- Make your strategy as open ended as possible. Creative people need a lot of freedom to work. Heck, they may want to ignore the strategy completely. So make it easy for them to do so.

---

# VI How to write contact reports

What's the most universal problem with contact reports? Their length.

They tell more than they need - probably because many writers do not understand the purpose of contact reports.

Contact reports have but one role in life—to record the decisions made at a meeting or through a telephone conversation and to specify the next steps to be taken.

They *do not* summarize the debate that preceded the decision.

They should *not* be used to build a case or to protect the agency from client recriminations. If such unfortunate action must be taken, the proper way is through a supplementary memo or letter.

So, the first rule for more effective contact report writing is to include only the decisions that were made at the meeting and the next steps that must be taken.

Here are four other tips to help you write better contact reports.

## 1. Be timely

Your report should be delivered within 48 hours of the meeting or telephone conversation.

## 2. Use clear headings. Use them frequently

More headings should be used in a contact report than in any other form of business writing. Use them to identify each discrete topic or decision area.

In a memo or letter, one topic may lead to another and you can use a bridging paragraph to connect the two. Since your contact report is really a series of telegrams announcing decisions, bridging paragraphs have no place and headings must be used.

## 3. Indicate action

Always identify who is responsible for implementing the decisions taken — by name rather than by work unit. And be sure to specify when the action must be completed.

However, don't rely on your contact report to initiate the action. That is not its purpose. Follow up with a proper briefing on what must be done. The contact report simply puts everyone on the alert to the need for action. You must still give the actual orders to fire.

## 4. Edit your distribution list

Do this at least once a year. Ask the people receiving your reports if they wish to continue being on the distribution list.

Even with your revised list, use some discretion.

Don't automatically send every report to everyone on your list. Send only those reports that will be of interest to your recipients.

The agency president does not need to know the brand manager agreed to remove the mole on the model's nose by retouching the photo.

---

**Three Ways To Make Contact Reports Useless**

- Make sure they're late, say, a couple of weeks after the event. Your readers will see your report as old news and toss it away.
- Report on everything that went on during the meeting or phone call in excruciating detail. No one will want to devote the time needed to read such a long report.
- Do not indicate who was to initiate the agreed upon action. If no one is identified no one can be held responsible.

---

# VII How to write store check reports

Store check reports are often the most superficial documents account people write. Unfortunately, this means that an opportunity has been lost to gain valuable insights about the client's brand and the competition it faces.

How? By turning the store check into a Know The Consumer project.

When doing a store check, don't just count facings, record prices and note in-store activity. Get beyond the numbers and talk to consumers as they buy your brand or your competitor's.

Here's a chance to understand consumers right at the decision point.

And while you're at it, talk to the store manager as well. He's one of your brand's must important consumers.

Ask him about the number of facings he gives your brand versus competitive brands. Or about shelf position, turnover rates, consumer complaints—or any number of other questions that will give you a better insight into your brand's performance. Then incorporate his comments plus those of the consumers into your report.

Your report should be set out in four sections:

- **Background**
- **Conclusions**
- **Indicated Action**
- **Details**

Let's cover them one by one.

**Background:** Here you'll record the basic details of your store check:

- Its purpose
- Where and when it was conducted
- The number of stores visited
- Their size range
- The number of consumers and store managers interviewed

**Conclusions:** This section contains your main observations and the conclusions you've drawn from them.

Where possible, show how your conclusions support (or perhaps contradict) other observations, beliefs or research findings.

**Indicated action:** Tell your reader what should be done based on the conclusions you've come to. As always, specify who should be responsible for the action and when it should be initiated.

**Details:** Summarize the findings for your brand and competitive brands in terms of:

- Distribution
- Facings
- Shelf position
- Pricing
- In-store promotions
- Consumer comments
- Store Manager's comments

Keep your report short and to the point.

But, importantly, get behind the numbers, into the minds of consumers.

**Three Ways to Make Your Store Check Reports Short (And Their Shelf Life Even Shorter)**

- Just tally up and report the numbers. Exclude any insights gleaned from consumers, store employees or store managers. Anecdotal comments might prompt the reader to relate your findings to important things like strategy or positioning, rather than concentrating on the shelf prices and distribution ratios you've recorded.

- Report the data collected on a store-by-store basis. Maybe on a chain-by-chain basis. But don't go further than that. Even if there are dots waiting to be connected, leave that for someone else to do. Why generalize when you don't have to?

- And resist the temptation to put the report in the context of brand and competitive marketing activity. Who's to say the competitor's price reduction had any effect on the brand's end-of-quarter promotion. Or that the out-of-stock levels may be related to the advertising heavy up.

# VIII How to write competitive copy reports

Competitive copy reports rank next to store check reports for superficiality. They usually consist of a one-paragraph letter to which a storyboard is attached. They fail to live up to their purpose, which is to:

- Determine the copy strategy the competition is using.
- Assess their strategy based on current research.
- Describe the advertising being used to execute the strategy.
- Assess the effectiveness of the advertising.
- Indicate what action should be taken.

The format for the copy report should be as follows.

Start by stating where the commercial or advertisement ran, how long it has been running, and whether it represents a national, regional or test campaign.

Then, construct the copy strategy you think the competition is using. Who's the target audience? What's the source of volume? What problem is this advertising trying to solve? What benefit is your competitor promising? What support is he offering?

Here's a chance for some perceptive deductive thinking!

Next, assess this strategy based on existing research or any other information you have. Is the competitor claiming an important benefit or an inconsequential one? Has he developed new and unique support for a benefit that was previously seen as generic? Do you think he's developed new insights about the market? What are these? And what are the strengths and weaknesses of his strategy?

In the third section of your report, describe the advertising your competitor is using. What is the selling idea and theme line? Is there a key visual? What type of executional format is being used?

Briefly describe all pertinent executional devices—from music to mnemonics.

With the executional description completed, you're ready to give your assessment of the advertising.

Does it execute the strategy effectively?

In your judgment is it memorable? Credible? Persuasive?

Does the quality speak well of the advertiser?

Involve your creative partners when preparing this section. They can be of great help.

Resist the temptation to denigrate your competition when writing your assessment. While your report will necessarily be subjective, it should be unbiased.

Your competitors are not stupid. They may have developed an insight you've missed.

The final section of your report deals with the action to be taken.

- Diagnostic research on the competitive execution?
- Supplementary research to evaluate the new strategic direction they are taking?
- The development and testing of a similar strategy for your brand?

Keep the initiative!

**Three Ways to Make Your Competitive Copy Reports Disposable**

- Be disdainful of the competition. They're the enemy; of course they're not as smart as you and the brand team. Nothing they do could be effective. Keep morale up by putting them down.
- Parse out the strategy but stay away from executional elements In particular, don't try to describe or evaluate the basic idea. It's all so subjective anyway.
- Above all else, don't relate the competitor's effort to your brand's copy. First, that's a lot of work. Secondly, someone might get the idea that your copy could be improved and that's really a lot of work.

# IX   How to write a deck

Done right, presentation decks can be one of the most effective communications tools available to you. Done wrong, they're a disaster. Why? Because done wrong, they (with your help) will bore your audience, if not put them to sleep. And whatever it was you were trying to achieve will go unachieved.

Here are ten tips to help you avoid disaster and get the most out of this ubiquitous device.

## 1.  Remember, your deck is just a prop

A presentation deck is just barely a form of written communications. It's really a presentation aide—a prop. Most of your presentation will be oral, or at least it should be.

The purpose of the deck is simply to help you and your audience stay focused and on track. It is not meant to be a written record of what you say.

## 2. The old rules still apply

If you're presenting a recommendation, the rules for writing recommendations still apply. If you're presenting a strategy, the rules for writing a strategy still apply.

Decks must be prepared with the same attention to the logical flow of your thoughts and arguments that you give to written communications. The major difference is that, with a deck, your writing will be much more succinct.

## 3. Use the tell'em rule

That's the rule that says, "Tell'em what you're going to tell'em. Tell'em. Then tell'em what you've told'em."

In other words, give your audience an outline of what you are going to present, ensure that the content adheres to the outline, and then end with a strong summary of what you have said.

If you follow this rule, you're chances for successful communication will increase immeasurably.

## 4. One page, one thought

This may be the most violated rule of all.

The purpose of a deck is to help your audience grasp the essence of what you are telling them orally. If you have multiple thoughts on the same page, they might focus on the wrong thought at the wrong time, become confused and miss the point you are trying to make.

This doesn't mean you can't have sub points elaborating on or supporting the main thought. You can and should. But these must be extensions of the main thought, not new ones.

## 5. No sentences please

The words you put on the page of a deck should not become sentences.

They should only be telegraphic signposts summarizing the essence of your point. In addition to giving your audience a heads up on what you're about to tell them, they jog your memory about what you plan to say and help the audience keep the point in mind as you elaborate on it orally.

If the words turn into sentences, the audience will read them rather than listen to what you are saying. And because they can read faster than you can speak, they'll be finished before you, conclude that you've communicated all they need to know about this point and quietly disengage from the presentation.

The nodding heads you're likely to then see are not nods of agreement. They're nodding off!

# 6. Read what's on the page

Read the signposts exactly as they are written. If you ad lib here, you risk confusing your audience.

Reading the signpost word for word helps your audience grasp the thought quickly; they hear and see your point simultaneously. You can then safely elaborate knowing they will be able to follow your train of thought easily.

# 7. Let charts speak for themselves

Well-designed charts and graphs are great communications aides. But don't dilute their power by summarizing in written words next to them what they are saying graphically.

If a summary is needed, it's better to do it orally, perhaps while pointing to the pertinent section of the graph or highlighting it with a laser beam.

# 8. Give your audience a road map

Your audience can easily lose track of where they are in your presentation. Are we still in the background section? Are these the conclusions?

A simple way to help your audience is to put the relevant section heading in the upper left hand corner of each page. If you can devise interesting symbols to represent each section, that's even better.

# 9. One page, one minute

When estimating the length of your presentation a good rule of thumb is to assume one minute for every page of your deck.

So if you have a sixty-page deck but only twenty minutes on the agenda, you've got some serious cutting to do. Getting rid of all those sentences and paragraphs is a good place to start.

## 10. Use a little show business

Unlike a written document, a presentation deck allows you to inject some pizzazz into your communication, if that's appropriate.

Fundamentally, you are trying to persuade your audience.

People are more easily persuaded by people they know and like than by people they don't know or don't like. So let your personality shine through. Include some unexpected element or device.

But don't over do it. This is not happy hour.

---

**Three Ways to Have Your Presentations Flop**

- Make your full, unabridged script the copy for your presentation deck. Read every word and even those in your audience who have had a good night's sleep will be anesthetized.
- Give out copies of the deck at the start of the meeting. That way people can save time by reading ahead if they like rather than just listening to you.
- Speak for every second of your allotted time and don't worry if you go over. If there's no time for discussion at the end of your presentation, those with serious questions can always catch up with you later.

---

# X   How to write e-mails, memos, and general correspondence

Most of your business writing will not consist of analyses, recommendations or strategies. Rather, the majority of your writing will be general letters, memos and e-mails asking for or giving information.

This correspondence is so common you probably give it little thought. And that's the problem.

Your lack of thought can result in wasted time and effort.

Let's take an example.

You write an e-mail giving direction on a project. But your direction isn't complete, or your thoughts are not sufficiently specific.

Consequently, the recipient of your memo misinterprets what you want. The result is a number of false starts, considerable frustration and many unproductive hours of work.

The general tips given in the first section will help combat this problem.

Here are six more suggestions to increase the productivity of your general correspondence.

## 1.  Get to the point, quickly

The productivity of most business writing could be improved immediately by following one simple rule:

> *State the purpose of your letter or memo in the first paragraph. Preferably, state it in the first sentence.*

That one change would eliminate the time wasted by your reader in speculating about your purpose.

With e-mails, be sure the subject heading you use is unambiguous and instantly tells the recipient what your e-mail is all about. You wouldn't want your e-mail to be left unread because your purpose in writing it was unclear.

## 2. Get to the point, and stay there

The next best way to boost productivity is by sticking to your subject.

Don't clutter up your memos with unnecessary information.

Don't tell your readers all you know. They're not interested!

Tell them only what they must know to understand what you want them to understand, follow your direction, or give you the information you require. Pretend you have to write your memo on a post card.

## 3. Be personable

Reveal yourself in your writing.

Advertising is a person-to-person business. Formula letters, memos and e-mails have no place.

A letter is something you send when you can't be there in person.

It's a substitute, but it should be close to the real thing.

## 4. Cause action

Be sure your e-mails or letters make things happen.

When summing up, specify what action you want taken, by whom and by when.

Be polite, but be assertive.

And when you've asked someone to do something, always have him or her advise you when they've completed the task.

When the responsibility for action falls to you, tell your readers exactly what your next steps are and when you'll update them on the status of the project.

## 5. Be courteous

Spell your reader's name correctly and get the title right.

If your reader uses two initials (many people do) make sure you have them correct.

## 6. End with emphasis

Stamp out wishy-washy endings such as, *"If you have any questions, please do not hesitate to call."* Unless your reader is a moron, of course he'll call if he has questions.

It's better to say *"I'll call you in a few days to see if you have any questions."* That way, you take the initiative and control the action.

Then, of course, do what you said you'd do.

---

**Three Ways To Make it Easy To Delete Your Emails**

- Write with a "stream of consciousness" style. Put down one thought after another, in any order, just as they pop into your head. It will seem as if you're right there speaking to the reader.
- Forget about punctuation, grammar and sentence structure. This will give your email a "hurried" appearance; as if what you have to say is so important you don't have time to follow the rules.
- Use acronyms. Lots of them. And hip text messaging shorthand like FWIW, AFAIC or @TEOTD. This will show you're, well, hip! Hip is good.

---

# XI  How to write a speech

Sooner or later, you'll be asked to give a speech. At first, you'll beam because your genius has been recognized, or at least your expertise in a particular area. You'll envision yourself at the podium, articulately conveying your thoughts and receiving a round of well-deserved applause at the end.

But then reality will intrude. You'll remember how nervous you became at the boss's birthday party last year when you had to propose the toast. Next, you'll realize that, of the hundred or so people likely to be in the audience, you will only know a few. And, most unsettling of all, you'll think, "What, exactly, am I going to say?"

And that's the first rule for writing an effective speech: Have something to say.

It seems self-evident but it's not as simple as that. The person who asked you to speak most likely will have given you a topic. While this may be what he or she would like you to talk about, it may not be what you should talk about. The topic may be too bland, too shallow, too esoteric or just too impractical. If that's the case, either decline the invitation or suggest an alternative topic—something related to theirs but one you feel you can deliver in an informative way.

Perhaps their topic is fine but you don't have the expertise in the area that they think you do. Another good reason to decline. Or perhaps their topic is fine, but you have one that you think is more interesting and equally appropriate for the audience. Try to persuade the host on the merits of your topic.

When you give a speech, your reputation is on the line. Consequently, it's critical that you speak on a subject that has substance and audience appeal; and one that interests you sufficiently that you'll commit the time and energy necessary to write and deliver an informative point of view. So let's modify the first rule stated above to:

# 1. Have something to say that's worth saying.

While there's no empirical data, it's a good bet that 80% of all speeches given should not have been.

# 2. Give a second thought to starting with a joke.

Yes, those who tell you how to make a speech talk about connecting with the audience quickly and getting a laugh is one way to do it. But comedy is tricky. And finding a new joke that's relevant to your topic or the occasion isn't easy. Then there's timing. Comedians will tell you timing is everything. So unless you're a gifted raconteur, it may be better to take a different approach. (Of course, this doesn't exclude a little lighthearted repartee with the host or audience before you begin your speech.)

Instead of a joke, write the opening of your speech as you'd write a newspaper headline. Grab your audience's attention with a thought-provoking fact, idea or observation. Even if the point is something you won't cover in detail until later in your speech, you can still use it as an opener by saying "Did you know that XXX? I'll elaborate more on this later, but first let me tell you about YYY". You've connected with your audience and given them a reason to pay attention. You're on a roll.

# 3. Do some original research.

This doesn't mean fielding a quantitative study. It means supporting the thoughts or ideas you're expressing through the collaboration of others. It may be as simple as talking with three or four colleagues about your topic and incorporating their thoughts, with attribution, into your speech. Or you could send an email to a dozen or so people, knowledgeable about your topic, asking them a series of brief questions.

Yes, that would be a very unscientific survey, but you're not seeking scientific accuracy. You're seeking anecdotal support for your views. Another approach is to comb relevant media for supporting statements made by others and include these in your speech. Anything you can do to show that your point of view is more than just one man's, or one woman's, opinion will be useful.

## 4. Give extra attention to the middle....and the end.

No matter how well written (and delivered) your speech is, at some point, the audience's attention will sag. Often, the biggest drop in attention occurs towards the middle of the speech. When writing, be sure to provide an "attention jolt" at this critical juncture. Just as you did at the opening, include a fact, idea, thought or opinion that will reconnect you and the audience.

There's usually a similar marked drop in attention towards the end of a speech. Plan another "attention jolt" there as well. And when you've finished writing, look the speech over carefully to see if there are other obvious spots where attention is likely to sag and rewrite accordingly.

## 5. Use rhetorical questions?

The answer is "yes". Rhetorical questions are a great device for connecting with the audience. People almost automatically pay more attention when asked a question, even a rhetorical one. But don't over do it. Like any device, less is more.

## 6. Put figures on charts.

It's difficult for an audience to comprehend large amounts of numerical data delivered orally. If you need to include such data, put the figures (using very large type) on a couple of charts. Obviously, this won't work very well if you are speaking to an audience of a thousand. In that case, it's best to rethink the use of the data. A slew of spoken numbers is sure to cause the audience's eyes to glaze over.

## 7. Keep your speech to 15 minutes.

If you write it for 15 minutes, it will be 20 minutes long when you give it. In fact, it will be closer to 30 minutes by the time you're introduced, walk to the podium, adjust the microphone and take a sip of water. Few, if any, ever complain about a speech being too short. But a speech that's too long? Well, you know how that goes.

## 8. Leave time for questions.

Another reason for adhering to the 15-minute rule when writing a speech is to allow time to have a dialogue with the audience. The questions asked will tell you what aspects of your speech were of greatest interest You can then elaborate on these in your responses. Tell the audience at the outset that you'll welcome their questions at the end of the speech (don't take questions during the speech; it's too distracting.) This is also a good way of connecting with the audience early.

Most of the suggestions made elsewhere in this book apply equally to writing speeches. And the specific tips given here don't touch on the important topic of how to give a speech. There are many useful books on this subject. If there's a thread running through the suggestions given above it is this: Writing a speech is not just about expressing what you want to say; it's also about getting the audience to listen.

# XII Summary

Now it's up to you.

You are the only person who can improve your writing ability.

Here are two final suggestions to help you do this.

The first thing you should do is practice.

As is the case with all skills, there is no substitute for practice.

Once a week, take a letter or recommendation you've written previously and re-write it following the guidelines given in this booklet. Then, compare the two versions.

You'll be amazed, and pleased, at the difference.

Every third day, take one of your e-mails or contact reports and do the same thing. Just one month of such practice will cause a significant improvement in your writing ability.

The second thing you should do is read.

To paraphrase the nutritionalists' cliché about being what we eat, "You are what you read."

By nature, human beings are imitators. Consciously or unconsciously we pick up the accents, mannerisms and styles of those around us. So if your reading consists of trashy novels, or if you forego reading in favor of sitcoms, chances are you'll talk and write like a TV character.

But if your entertainment menu includes quality novels, biographies, and well-written works on topics of substance, your writing will begin to reflect the style of these more accomplished authors.

When you think about it, writing is one of the few skills you can improve by doing something pleasurable.

As an agency account manager, one of your most important responsibilities (I think *the* most important responsibility) is to persuade others: to persuade your agency colleagues in various departments, for example, to assign their resources to meet your client's needs; to persuade your client of the validity of your agency's recommendations.

Sometimes you can persuade others by dint of your personality. But often you'll need something more.

That "something" is a well-reasoned argument, succinctly stated. The writing tips in this guide will help you develop and articulate such persuasive arguments.

As stated at the beginning, good writing skills are a prerequisite for success in advertising. This guide will help you succeed.

Finally, keep in mind what Hemingway had to say about writing:

> *"There's no rule on how it is to write. Sometimes it comes easily and perfectly. Sometimes it is like drilling rock and then blasting it out with charges."*

# XIII    Bibliography

Here's a list of books for those who wish to learn more about effective writing.


*The Elements of Style*

William Strunk, Jr. and E.B. White


*On Writing Well*

William Zinsser


*The Classic Guide To Better Writing*

Rudolf Flesch and A.H. Lass


*The Art of Readable Writing*

Rudolph Flesch


*How To Write, Speak and Think More Effectively*

Rudolph Flesch


*Writing that Works*

Kenneth Roman and Joel Raphaelson

# About the Author

Norm MacMaster is a retired agency executive who spent the bulk of his career with the J Walter Thompson Company. He began his career in account management then progressed to general management responsibilities in North America and Japan, regional management responsibilities in Asia, and global management responsibilities for two of JWT's top five clients. He was a member of the agency's board of directors and also served on the Worldwide Executive Committee. Norm lives with his wife Maureen in Rye, New York. No longer involved in the fast-paced world of advertising, Norm is enjoying the slower-paced world of sailing and cruising in the Northeast and the Caribbean.